MMO
3846

T0078541

ALEXANDER ARUTIUNI

CONCERTO

ALEXANDER GOEDICKE

CONCERT ÊTUDE

for Trumpet
and
Symphonic Wind Ensemble

To access audio visit:
www.halleonard.com/mylibrary

3707-8882-1021-9315

ISBN 978-1-59615-099-7

Music Minus One

EXCLUSIVELY DISTRIBUTED BY

HAL•LEONARD®

7777 W. BLUEMOUND RD. P.O. BOX 13819 MILWAUKEE, WI 53213

Visit Hal Leonard Online at
www.halleonard.com

NOTES ON THE RECORDING

On this recording I have performed both works on a La Tromba "Mark V" piston-valve trumpet (with a copper bell and lead pipe, in 24-karat gold-plate).

The tone character of this trumpet is similar to an American-made Vincent Bach "Stradivarius" model with a medium-large bore of 11.5mm or .460; but because of the special "resonating plates" that I have built into the bow of the bell and tuning slide in this model (the plates, too, are made of pure copper), the heavy mouthpiece receiver and valve-caps combined with the La Tromba "Heavy" Mouthpiece (with an 18.5 mm cup diameter and a 4.1 mm bore), it is a very much more powerful trumpet than any factory-built model on the market today.

This instrument's extraordinary power comes from its extreme focus of sound and intensity—this in both dynamic extremes—and is, by anyone's standards, truly a "soloist's instrument." It has a very compact and extremely "directional" tone-center that allows the performer to easily dominate any orchestra and wind ensemble. Because one can much more easily play both very quietly and very, very loudly without distorting or losing the tone substance, it is however very difficult to record even using the highest quality of microphones available today. I therefore would like to thank Mr. Boris Archimovich, the head recording technician, for his extra efforts during these Kiev recording dates.

I would also like to thank the members of the State Wind Orchestra of the Ukraine and its conductor, Mr. Alexi Roschak, for their tireless work in the numerous rehearsals preceding the recordings in the National Philhamonie of Kiev from May 10th to the 12th, 2003 (during which a freak heat wave took the temperature in the recording studio well over 100 degrees Fahrenheit!) and my friend and colleague Mr. Valery Posvaliuk, Solo Trumpeter of the National Opera of Kiev for his organizational help for these recordings in Kiev. Last but not least, I would like to thank Mr. Alexander Klebel of Marell Studios in Würzburg, Germany. With his extraordinary patience and expert knowledge of sound engineering, he helped immeasurably with the mastering of these recordings in June of 2003.

Recorded 10-12 May 2003, National Philharmonie of Kiev, Ukraine
Richard Carson Steuart, soloist
State Wind-Orchestra of the Ukraine
Alexi Roschak, Conductor
Engineer: Boris Archimovich
Mastered at Marell Studios, Würzburg, Germany
Mastering Engineer: Alexander Klebel
Audio Producer: Richard Carson Steuart

Music Minus One

3846

CONTENTS

ALEXANDER ARUTIUNIAN
TRUMPET CONCERTO

Andante maestoso 6

ALEXANDER GOEDICKE
CONCERT ÊTUDE

Allegro molto 19

Alexander Arutiunian
Trumpet Concerto in A♭
(Version for Trumpet in B♭ and Symphonic Wind Ensemble)

This concerto was composed in 1950 and, although it was first published in 1956, it was not premiered until 1960, when it was performed in Moscow by the Armenian trumpeter Aikas Mesiyan accompanied by the Moscow State Symphony Orchestra.

ALEXANDER GRIGORI ARUTIUNIAN (his last name being pronounced: Harut´unian) was born in Everan, Armenia in 1921. He graduated from the Everan Music Conservatory in 1941 and continued his compositional studies in Moscow at the "House of Armenian Studies" from 1946 to 1948 under Litinsky, Peyko and Tsukkerman. It was in fact his work "Kantate Hayerenikimasin" (Cantate of the Homeland) written as his graduation piece from that "Conservatory" in Moscow that earned Arutiunian his first international recognition and this at the very beginning of his compositional career!

Most of his earlier compositions written through to the late 1950s are, as is this trumpet concerto, based on traditional Armenian folk-melodies thus revealing his strong nationalistic tendencies and his affinity to his more famous countryman Aram Khachaturian, who is undoubtedly best known for his dramatic musical description of an Armenian "Saber Dance."

The trumpet virtuoso Aikas Mesiyan (born 1917) studied with the famous Professor Tabakov at the Moscow "Tchaikovsky" Conservatory. After completing his studies he became a member of the world famous Bolshoi Theater Orchestra and at the end of the 2nd World War returned to his homeland Armenia where he later met and inspired Alexander Arutiunian to write this Concerto and dedicate it to him.

The final cadenza that I have performed on this recording was written by the now world famous Ukranian trumpeter Timofey Dokschitzer (born 1921). Dokschitzer, too, is a former member of the Bolshoi Theater Orchestra as both Solo Trumpeter and Conductor, and is widely considered to be one of the most artistic and virtuoso trumpet soloists of all time. First brought to the attention of the American public in 1970 by then-professor of trumpet at the Indiana University, Louis Davidson, Dokschitzer's phe-nomenal recordings, not only of this concerto but of many other works, including those originally for violin by Fritz Kreisler, Pablo Sarasate and Dinicu-Heifetz, clearly display his phenomenal technique and musical artistry.

Musicians of Timofey Dokschitzer's caliber are always an important inspiration for young music students and an important factor in their musical development. I can certainly say that, parallel to the charismatic and flamboyant Mexican-American trumpet virtuoso Rafeal Méndez, Timofey Dokschitzer was my greatest inspiration as a young trumpeter growing up in a quiet Western Canadian city in the late 1960s.

✣

The Arutiunian Trumpet Concerto itself is a one movement work structured in a series of rhapsodic "episodes" each continuing *attacca* (that is, without a formal

pause in the music) from section to section. The work requires both emotional depth and high technical ability of the performer to be played in a convincing manner. To be sure of perfect technical control through the work I suggest that the very fast passages should be practiced very slowly at first, taking care to execute each section of the work with a relaxed and yet exact rhythm and a very steady pulse. Many of the difficult "double-tonguing" passages may take many hours of practice to master. But remember the old axiom, "practice slowly and you will learn quickly!" I often remind my students that when they are learning a new musical work, they should never let a mistake go by without its immediate correction, otherwise one will find he has in fact practiced a mistake!

Beginning with a powerfully dramatic cadenza-like prelude marked *Andante maestoso* (moderately slow and majestically), the work instantly holds the listener's attention. A distinctly Armenian (or for our western ears an "eastern European") harmony and scale is used by the composer: notably one with the unusual interval of three half-tones from both the 3rd to 4th and from the 6th to 7th steps in the tonic scale. Arutiunian's application of traditional folk melodies over this "oriental" harmony creates a truly exotic atmosphere which I feel can easily be compared with Rimsky-Korsakov's famous *"Scheherazade" Suite Symphonique*, op. 35.

The work has an intensive almost urgent musical message which is demonstrated from the very beginning of the work as the trumpet seems to "call out" to the listener, telling a tale or even a "legend" of heroic dimension.

Articulations in the work are, I believe, a question of tempo and individual technical ability and should be seen from this perspective. Although written with a "phrasing bow" and therefore performed often with a "slur," I have deliberately chosen to double-tongue this first scale-passage from low C to High A-flat in bar 12, simply to emphasize its percussive, dramatic intensity. The passage is marked with both *an accelerando* (gradually faster) and at the same time *tenuto* (meaning broadly) which may seem a contradiction in terms, but in fact it is not at all, because broad notes (those played with full rhythmic value) can nevertheless be played very quickly and clearly, and thus convey even more intensity than shorter notes, and can at the same time be given more dynamic contour. For this reason I suggest the young performer attempt to give "full value" to each note in every phrase, whether at slow or fast tempo. This does not, of course, mean that the tones should be tongued less clearly, however, as is often the mistake when performing in such a manner.

After the dramatic introduction the work quickly moves to the first thematic section marked *Allegro energico* (fast and with energy). An intensive rhythmic nine-bar ensemble introduction prepares for the trumpet's first exciting melody. It is in my view clearly a "riding" theme somewhat similar in character to the percussive groups of double tongued sixteenth notes in third movement of the Johann Nepomuk Hummel Concerto in E major, or in Suppe´s "William Tell" Overture but full of exciting syncopated accents and interval jumps.´ When performing this work I often try to envisage heroic, historical personalities such as the famous Cossack leader Taras Bulba of the Ukrainian Steppe, riding at the front of his nomadic folk to their legendary battles to regain their freedom from the then occupying Polish armies.

Envisioning such heroic deeds and persons may not be possible for everyone when performing such music and undoubtedly requires an extra degree of imagination from the individual, but it has always been an aid for me when trying to grasp and then portray the musical intensity of a work of this kind.

The second major section of the concerto is marked *Meno mosso* and begins with a slow and expressive clarinet solo. The same lyrical, introverted melody is then taken over by the solo trumpet and should, I believe, be performed with great dynamic variance and a controlled but expressive vibrato. A tasteful *rubato (*defined as *"robbing the tempo")* can also be applied here, but such a concept is not easily described in words nor performed convincingly without practice. Varying the tempo of the melody without losing contact with the steady pulse of the accompaniment is a technique that allows an extra freedom within each phrase helping to emphasize the most expressive portions of each individual musical idea. This is where listening to mature musical performers can be a great help as a guide to every developing performer.

At Letter E the trumpet's line becomes a complementary voice to the melody or an *obligato* line, and begins its dialogue with the entire ensemble. The trumpet should not attempt to compete in dynamics with the ensemble melody but only enhance it. Only in the 12th bar of this section marked *animato* should the trumpet be briefly allowed to show its fortissimo power before again taking the subservient role in the musical dialogue.

A woodwind interlude follows, leading straight into an abrupt tempo change at Letter G marked *Tempo I*. This section of the work is dominated by an agitated and fragmented melodic dialogue between the trumpet and various members of the woodwind ensemble, modulating harmonically several times as it sets it dialogue forth.

I feel it is important that the trumpet not play too loudly here; that is, that the performer stays in proper balance to each of the woodwind instruments in turn but at the same time maintains his soloistic intensity and clarity in preparation for the next abrupt change of musical character at Letter H marked *cantando*. Here trumpet soloist should be careful not to lose tempo in the short lyrical sections interspersed, since he must repeatedly jump back and forth from the agitated to the *cantando* theme throughout this section. It ends suddenly with a final double-tongued chromatic *fortissimo crescendo* into the next orchestral interlude at Letter L.

The orchestra is then allowed over the next thirty-four bars to develop the thematic material to its full dynamic capacity. Both trumpets and trombones compete for melodic dominance in waves of ascending diatonic phrases, until once again—eleven bars before letter M—this all ends quite abruptly at the high point of its intensity, and the solo clarinet repeats the introverted and mournful first theme presented in the introduction of the work accompanied by *sordino* trumpets.

This short interlude prepares for the next *meno mosso* solo section marked *con sordino* and again *cantando*. The ensemble trumpets begin a muted two-bar syncopated introduction using the so-called cup- mute to soften their sound for an added "veiled" effect. The soloist, too, is required to play with a mute by the composer and should choose one that sets his tone character apart from sound of the accompanying trumpets. Any number of *sordino* or "mutes" can be used to alter the tone character of the trumpet, ranging from the "Harmon" mute (with or without the stem) over "Robinson" to the standard straight mute in cardboard wood or metal. I have chosen to use a very special "Solo-tone" mute made in the 1930s that I was very fortunate to acquire when purchasing a very rare vintage pre-First World War English *Boosey and Co.* cornet. This specific mute is made of cardboard and wood and has an extended resonating tube. It makes a very gentle and subtle, almost woodwind-like, sound that I believe speaks to the character of the music in this section of the concerto.

The trumpet melody here is in dialogue with the euphonium (or in the case of this recording, the Bassoon) and should be played tastefully and with grace, taking care not to exaggerate the syncopated portions of the melody, especially in the fourth and again in the sixth bars before letter N. From here on, its possible to be a little more free with the tempo of the melody and perform with more *rubati,* but always be careful not to go to extremes and become "schmalzig" (to use an old German expression, describing an emotional exaggeration...that is, to the point of what we might call tastelessness). After a brief orchestral interlude and *ritardando* before Letter O the soloist must again lead the musical dialogue ending four bars before Letter P in a long *diminuendo*. The clarinet once again plays the interim melody leading to Letter P at which time a somewhat extended version of the introduction to the first theme as at Letter A is presented by the orchestra leading to the recapitulation of the first theme now marked simply *Tempo I*. This section of the work ends in an extended double-tongued transitional scale passage in the solo part leading directly to the final cadenza.

The cadenza performed on this recording, as I have mentioned earlier, was written by the world-famous Ukrainian trumpeter Timofey Dokschitzer who, I believe, is truly a master of cadenza composition and this in many styles as can be heard on several his own excellent recordings. Dokschitzer masterfully uses key thematic material and exciting technical elements of the work to prepare for the intensive final bars of the concerto accompanied by the orchestra. I believe his cadenza is an excellent ending to this important composition of the modern "classical" trumpet repertoire.

—*Richard Carson Steuart*

CONCERTO

for B♭ Trumpet
and Symphonic Wind Ensemble

Alexander Arutiunian
arr. Guy M. Duker

One measure of taps (4 taps) precedes music

8

10

Alexander Goedicke
Concert Être, op. 49
(Version for Solo Bb Trumpet and Symphonic Wind Ensemble)

ALEXANDER FYODOROVICH GOEDICKE (1877-1957) was of German descent and came from a traditional musical family with **Friedrich Alexander Paul Goedicke**, his father, as both organist and pianist in the Bolshoi Theater in Moscow.

Goedicke himself studied the piano at the Moscow Conservatory. Although a widely respected musician and teacher in his day, he reportedly did not study composition formally. Nevertheless he won the Rubinstein Composition Prize in Vienna in 1900 for his Concert Piece for piano, op. 2/2, written in 1896.

In 1909 he became professor for piano at the Moscow Conservatory, with his duties being further extended in 1919 to include instruction in both organ and chamber music at the Conservatory. He is reported to have had a strong influence especially on organists of his generation in Russia, as well as in the entire Soviet Union.

Goedicke composed a diverse number of works from opera (four) to symphony (three in number) as well as numerous overtures and several chamber-music pieces. His compositional style was oriented on the German model, in which he also composed concerti for the piano, organ, violin, horn, as well as his dramatic single-movement Concerto for Trumpet, op. 41 (1930), a work which is regarded as an excellent example of early New-Romantic trumpet repertoire.

The Concert Être, originally written for solo trumpet with orchestral accompaniment, was composed in 1936 at a transitional time in the development of the National School for Russian trumpet performance. Up until this time the German and Czech schools and traditions of trumpet performance had dominated in Russia, this dating as far back as the mid-1800s. The most influential personalities in eastern Europe brass performance of these earlier times were the Czech trumpet virtuoso Josef Kail (1795-1871) of the Prague Conservatory (who in 1826 was appointed the first Professor of Trumpet in Europe) as well as German/Russian trumpeters and teachers such as Wilhelm Wurm (1826-1904), and most notably Willy Brandt (1869-1923). Each of these trumpeters performed exclusively on the rotary-valve or so called "German" trumpets and cornets of that time. Kail was in fact directly involved in the development of both the Vienna-valve (1823) and the rotary-valve (1835) in collaboration with the Viennese brass instrument-maker Joseph Riedl (+1840). (For more information, see Dr. Edward H. Tarr's forward to Kail's Variations for the Trumpet in (low) F (1827) printed by McNaughtan Music Publications, Coburg Germany.)

Even the famous Russian trumpet virtuoso Timofey Dokschitzer began his studies on the rotary-valve cornet (made by Alexander Brass instruments, Mainz Germany) and this very instrument is now a part of a large number of historic instruments that can be seen today in the famous Bad Säckingen Trumpet Museum in southern Germany.

Mikhail Tabakov (1877-1956), one of Willy Brandt's most successful students and his successor as solo-trumpeter in the Bolshoi Theater Orchestra in Moscow, was in fact the catalyst in the most radical change in the Russian school of trumpeting, namely the introduction of the piston-valve or "Périnet" valve instrument into the Russian orchestra.

Dr. Edward H. Tarr reports in his 1997 preface to his edition of this work, printed again by David McNaughtan..."In June 1934, a Russian delegation looking for high-quality instruments had just left New York. Vincent Bach (1890-1976) who had been building trumpets since 1924 and tenor and bass trombones since 1928, perceived a business opportunity. He followed the group to Europe with a B-flat trumpet and a tenor trombone. The Russian delegation was impressed, but they required Tabakov to have a longer opportunity to test the instruments under working conditions...more than a year later he (Vincent Bach) received an order for 36 trumpets and trombones."

It was Sergey Nikolayevich Yeriomin (1903-75), however, and not Tabakov, who premiered the Concert Être on a Perinet-valve trumpet in 1936 with Goedicke himself as his piano accompanist. This Duo-version was written by the composer three years after his original work for trumpet and orchestra and was first printed in 1939.

The German trumpet has since that time almost completely disappeared in Russia and is no longer played in any major symphony orchestra there. As a designer and builder of both rotary-valve and piston-valve trumpets, I have come to know and appreciate the qualities of both designs and their specific tone characters.

I have also had the honor of reintroducing this traditional German instrument in Russia and the Ukraine through a series of lectures and concerts at the Gnesin Institute and Tchaikovsky Conservatory in Moscow as well as the Rimsky-Korsakov Conservatory in St. Petersburg in 2000. I was invited to perform in a new series of concerts in the St. Petersburg Trumpet Festival in June 2004 in which, besides performing with Symphonic Wind Ensemble and Chamber Orchestra, I performed the Sonata of Paul Hindemith on a La Tromba rotary-valve trumpet in B-flat with piano accompaniment.

The Concert Être, although reportedly first performed by Mr. Yeriomin at a relatively slow tempo in 4, should I believe be played *alla breve* and at a brisk but steady tempo. Great dynamic range is necessary to underline the work's musical intensity and drama, and to prevent it from sounding in any way academic. The double-tonguing passages should not, however, interfere with the musical line of the work or compromise the extreme dynamic variance necessary to perform this short but exciting work convincingly. The *quasi cantabile* passages at Number 5 and Number 9 should be played very broadly and powerfully, but always in a "singing" style.

The short cadenza-like section starting four bars before Number 10 marked *pesante* (heavy), should I believe be played a dramatically and powerfully as possible but one should be careful not to slow down too much before the final *rallentando* bar, otherwise the section will become too heavy and spoil the recapitulation of the theme at the *a tempo* (Number 10). From here to the end of the work the tempo should remain very steady, with the ending being played very simply and quietly like a "whispered secret" quickly spoken in one's ear.

—*Richard Carson Steuart*

CONCERT ÊTUDE

for Bb Trumpet
and Symphonic Wind Ensemble
Op. 49

Alexander Goedicke
arr. Timothy Topolewski

One measure of taps (4 taps) precedes music

Allegro molto

TRUMPET IN Bb

22